The Grumpy Girl's Guide
to Good Manners

THE
GRUMPY GIRL'S GUIDE
TO GOOD MANNERS

by Rachel Aboukhair

New Chapter Publisher
Sarasota 2011

Published by New Chapter Publisher

ISBN 978-0-9827918-4-4

New Chapter Publisher
1765 Ringling Blvd.
Suite 300
Sarasota, FL 34236
tel. 941-954-4690
www.newchapterpublisher.com

The Grumpy Girl's Guide to Good Manners
is distributed by Midpoint Trade Books

Printed in the United States of America

Cover design and layout by Shaw Creative
www.shawcreativegroup.com

TO MOM

TABLE OF CONTENTS

THE Grumpy Girl's Guide

To Good Manners

PROLOGUE

I can be extremely unpleasant. I can be like those pictures of Beethoven with the crazy hair and the bushy eyebrows, scowling because I'm deaf or something.

I got this picture off the Internet for you to have as a reference point. That, in a nutshell, is my personality (minus the musical genius part). If I'm hearing-impaired—as my mom claims when I don't listen to her—it's probably because I played my iPod too loud for too long. But I *have* conquered the crazy hair bit with the help of a powerful flat iron.

I think I'm grouchy because I'm tall. My theory is that because tall girls are early bloomers, they go through a long, disturbingly awkward stage, which makes them grumpy in their teenage years. Also, they can get away with being grumpy (to a certain extent) because they tower over others and nobody wants to mess with them.

The best thing tall girls have going for them is they can wait for a modeling scout to spot them in the mall and sign them to a contract that will rocket them into supermodel stardom. That hasn't happened for me yet, but I wait ever so hopefully. The brilliancy of my plan lies in the fact that when I *do* become a famous supermodel, I can *still* continue to be an obnoxious twit-face (as it seems some supermodels are), and yet, at the same time, get paid an exorbitant amount of money to fly around the world, be dangerously thin, spark controversies, and at some point marry a famous athlete or movie star.

Anyway, while I'm waiting to be discovered, I spend most of my time standing awkwardly on the sidelines, mocking passers-by in my mind, or mocking them to their faces, which drives them away and I end up alone. The few friends I do have I never want to talk to, unless, of course, I'm around the people I actually don't like, in which case I do talk to my friends, so I can avoid the people I don't like. Got it? It's a very well-thought-out system!

For some reason my mom didn't consider this such an enlightened attitude—she accuses me of having social ineptitude (as if it were some kind of disease)—and decided I had to be reformed.

And where do parents send their rebellious children for improvement? Boarding school! Yes, but that's not where she sent me. I actually would have *preferred* that. Instead, she decided to ship me off to

—cue the lightning flash—

ETIQUETTE CAMP!!!!!

That's right. A week-long camp on etiquette in Nowheresville, Texas. You can imagine my horror.

Somehow I survived that ill-fated week, and here I am writing about it to share my misery with you. That I'm writing a satire goes without saying. My favorite satire to date is "Candide" by Voltaire (who, in my opinion, was too grouchy to be buried in the crypts at the Panthéon in Paris in the company of other distinguished writers and famous scientists. The crypts, by the way, are quite lovely.) I wonder if you have to be French to be buried in the Panthéon. I can be French. *Le singe est dans l'arbre. C'est un vrai cirque ici aujourd'hui.*

But I digress.

I don't really speak French, but even if I did, it wasn't going to get me out of the cruel and unusual punishment awaiting me. My mom was sending me to this manners boot camp in the middle of the desert "for my own good," and so to this place grumpily I went.

CHAPTER 1

THE HORROR! THE HORROR!

The beginning is always a good place to start, but I'm not going to do that since that would be in 1994 (when I was born). Instead, I will commence my tale June of 2009, the 15th year of my glorious existence, when my mother called me into her room.

Mom: *Rachel! Come here, I want to talk to you for a sec.*

Me: *Am I in trouble?*

Mom: *Should you be?*

Me: *Yeess—no—I don't know!*

Mom: *You know that etiquette camp I was telling you about?*

Me: *Yes…???*

In that millisecond it crossed my mind what she was about to say and, horrified, I froze in place.

Mom: You're going in two weeks.

Let me pause for a moment to explain. I know you're wondering what in the world is etiquette camp. If you're not, then you most likely have been to one, and I salute you. We veterans need to stick together. My mom heard about this place where you get lessons in proper manners and social behavior from a local etiquette teacher who had actually been to my house before to instruct me. Yes, that's right: an etiquette teacher who makes house calls. I guess my mom felt that the private lessons didn't "take" and figured a week-long immersion elsewhere was called for. So, essentially, she was punishing me with the two things I hate most in the world: proper conduct and people.

I screamed and yelled and gnashed my teeth (I didn't really—what is gnashing of teeth, anyway?). But I did cry, beg and barter. Moreover, I pouted, threatened, groveled and whimpered—all to no avail.

So, I tracked down my dad, who is a softie, to enlist his aid. He used to deliver babies for a living (he was an obstetrician, not a stork, in case you were confused) and you can't have that job unless you're all mushy and sweet on the inside. Although he usually defers to my mom in matters of "raising the children," I was able to convince him to plead my case.

He tried but Mom was having none of it. She insisted that I was only seeing the negative side of things and that I might actually enjoy it if I changed my attitude. Actually, enlisting Dad in my cause just made her mad, because I was not supposed to "try to circumvent" her rules. So she sent me to my room to contemplate my treacherous behavior. While I was contemplating (sure), I secretly got on the Internet to investigate this etiquette camp.

On the official website, *www.finaltouchschool.com,* the camp was actually called "Final Touch Finishing School." But I think that was just their way of euphemizing what it actually was: etiquette boot camp. I would have to spend a week at a ranch resort in—get this— Paradise, Texas, with other girls to learn all the life skills necessary to succeed. At least it wouldn't be coed. My social awkwardness amplifies x 10 around the opposite sex. More on that later.

I asked my mom if my older sister, Sarah, was coming to camp with me. Hey, if I had to go, so should she. Mom said no; Sarah didn't need etiquette lessons. It wasn't fair! I was going to be banished to this place for a week to learn "life skills," while she got to stay home. She always avoids the punishments assigned to me because she is oh-so-popular and oh-so-musical and so faboosh in general. I am but her younger, less talented, and less likeable sister.

Then I remembered that somewhere in that horrid initial conversation, my mom had informed me that she had called Aunt Mona, and her daughter Katie (my cousin) was coming, too. Initially, I was relieved. If I was going to be miserable, at least I would have someone with whom to share my misery.

But the more I thought about it, the less comfort it brought me. A *week*? With *Katie*?

Don't get me wrong. I love Katie, but only in small doses. You see, what with her non-stop gabbing, Ms. Katie Bell could best be described as a very large Furby. Those of you who have no idea what a Furby is, please refer to the illustration to the right.

My cousin Paul drew that. Not bad, eh?

Furbies were a brand of toys developed in the late 1990s. They were tiny, mechanical gremlins with voices, and occasionally you had to feed and tickle them. They looked harmless enough. At first, it was nice to hear them talk and laugh, and all that jazz, but after a while they would NOT shut up, and if you didn't feed them every five seconds they would start yelling, "Feed me! Feed me!" in an annoyingly piercing voice. And, since six-year-olds have better things to do than to feed tiny talking gremlins all day and there was absolutely no way to turn them off, you would have to resort to hiding them in places that would muffle the noise (like under your mattress). Then, when they finally fell asleep they would make loud snoring noises! Eventually, they became a total nightmare.

Katie didn't look like a Furby, she just acted like one: seemingly innocuous, but once you spent time with her, she wouldn't shut up—even when she was asleep—and you wished you could hide her under the mattress to drown out that high-pitched noise.

But Katie was the least of my worries. As I continued to peruse the website, I saw a list of the things we were going to learn. It included the following:

Dance Etiquette

Nutrition, Exercise

Posture for Health & Appearance

Wardrobe Planning & Building

Art of Thank You Notes

Tea Etiquette

Electronic Etiquette

Electronic etiquette? You mean how to deal politely with my computer? Tea etiquette? That would come in handy, I'm sure.

The only positive I could see from having to go to this punishment camp was that it'd get me away from Michael and John David, my younger brothers. They are wild and crazy and like to play Michael

Jackson CDs at 7 a.m. At least I would avoid that chaos for a week. See, I *do* know how to look at the positive end of things.

This momentary optimism abruptly ended when I read on the site that on the last night of camp there was going to be a "final dinner" where we could wear "anything from a simple dress to something more formal." It was promoted as "a fun opportunity to dress up." Oxymoron, anyone? But wait, there was more. "Each young lady should bring one pair of shoes with heels for visual poise."

Heels? No way were they ever going to get *me* in heels! And visual poise? What the heck was that? Mom, what have you gotten me into!?!

I went to an online dictionary to enlighten myself and read:

Visual - *adjective*

1. Of or pertaining to seeing or sight
2. Perceptible by the sense of sight; visible

Poise - *noun*

1. A state of balance or equilibrium, as from equality or equal distribution of weight
2. A dignified, self-confident manner of bearing

So, an equal distribution of weight perceptible by the sense of sight. Well, I'm glad that's cleared up.

The final part of the site warned that "all students are expected to uphold the standards of respect for self, others and property. Not doing so will result in a student being sent home *at their own expense.*" Eureka!! There *was* a way out! I just had to "disrespect someone's property." Maybe I could sass Katie's iPod or—I don't know— proposition the teacher's suitcase. Not sure what it'd be yet, but at least I had options.

18

CHAPTER 2

PARADISE?

We picked up Katie at the airport on our way to the etiquette camp. The last time I'd seen her she was about 5'6", light-skinned, with long, black, wavy hair and brown eyes, and that was exactly what she looked like when I saw her again at the baggage claim, except with a lot more eyeliner.

I was tired and cranky and didn't feel like making conversation. But that wasn't a problem because Katie was capable of holding an entire conversation all on her own. "Rachel, I missed you! It's so cooool we're going to camp together! Oh my gosh, the guy next to me on the plane was soooo good looking! I brought boots! How's Sarah? I can't wait until you see my new iTouch. I brought money so we could shop! Do you want to shop?"

On the 45-minute drive to Paradise, Katie wasted no time in catching me up with the goings-on in her life, in particular the soap opera of her relationship with her ex-boyfriend Logan (not his real name) who broke up with her for no apparent reason after *such* lovely three months together and everyone said they were *soooo* perfect for each other but he broke up with her just like THAT over the phone and only *one hour* afterwards he called to ask out Samantha, Katie's friend (not her real name either), and Samantha said YES—that little twit—how could he like *Samantha* anyway?

I couldn't take any more of the latest episode of "The Young and the Restless" and was about to scream when I fortunately remembered something I'd read somewhere: Technology is killing the art of conversation. So I reached for Katie's iTouch to tune her out and played "Scoops," "MazeFinger," and "Are You Smarter Than a 5th Grader?" for a quarter of an hour.

During the drive to my miserable fate, I realized three things:

1. I am indeed *not* smarter than a fifth grader.

2. Katie was very convincing in showing me that she was really over Logan by continually mentioning him and Samantha. Not.

3. Since Katie's iTouch had been so good to me by helping me avoid Katie's prattle, I couldn't possibly disrespect it as a means of escape. Not after all it had done for me.

After missing our exit and spending 15 minutes searching for the ranch sign that seemed hidden in the bushes, we finally arrived. The first thing I saw was horses, then I noticed the statues of cows and buffaloes, and lastly, a large wooden building rising from the dust. What instantly came to my mind was "Hotel California": either it would be heaven, or it would be hell; but with my track record, the latter was the more likely.

The three of us emerged from the car with our eyes squinting, thinking this *must* be the wrong place. The whole area was kind of abandoned-looking, sort of like those old western movies where two cowboys are fighting a duel in an old dusty town while Grace Kelly is taking the next train out. It occurred to me that the person responsible for naming the town "Paradise" was probably the same person responsible for naming Greenland and Madonna. It might have been con-sidered paradise in the Kalahari Desert, but I don't think anyone else would dream of calling it that.

When walking into the hotel lobby for registration, I inferred from the cowhide rugs and deer horn lamps that the property was Texas-themed. I'm brilliant that way. We waited to check in behind a loud, sunburned, middle-aged couple who acted like they could use a camp in etiquette as well.

When it was our turn, the receptionist asked, "Are you girls here for the camp?"

"Yes…"

She handed us two huge binders marked "Life Skills." Apparently this program was well-coordinated. I passed mine on to Mom, hoping she'd take it with her, but she flipped through it with a way-too-interested look before giving it back to me.

In the meantime, the receptionist had handed us our room keys. How quaint—they didn't have room cards like other, modern-day hotels.

The rooms were in a separate building across from the main lobby—a large, old, one-story, wooden structure. The boardwalk running alongside was decorated with faded-looking rocking chairs, sun-bleached animal bones and strange, antiquated lamps. Katie and

I were in room 68. I knew I wouldn't have any trouble remembering where it was, right by the cow skull and the Jesse James poster. *Really.*

The screen door moaned when I pulled it open, as if to warn me: "Turn back, Rachel! Get out while you can!"

I reluctantly took the key from my pocket, inserted it in the keyhole and tried to turn it to the right. It wouldn't budge, so I wiggled it harder and put all my weight into twisting it. Still nothing.

When I started to violently rattle the key and slam myself against the door in an attempt to shove it open, Katie interfered.

"Rachel, I got it. Look."

With one turn of the key to the left she gently pushed the door open. *Show off.*

The room smelled dusty and had two queen-sized beds with a dresser in between, a desk and a table. The style was Texas quaint. It wasn't five stars—or even three—but it was actually nice, much to my surprise. The bathroom had a closet and a shower (and a toilet, but I think that goes without saying).

My mom read some book that was left on the night stand about a guy who distracted himself from his OCD by watching a lot of movies while we unpacked. Wait. That wasn't a good grammatical sentence. It sounds like the guy watched movies while we unpacked. There was no guy. Let me rephrase that: While we unpacked, my mom read some book that was left on the night stand about a guy who distracted himself from his OCD by watching a lot of movies. Much better.

After unpacking I was instantly bored, so I wandered over to open the tired-looking, once-beige, lace curtains. I pulled them to the side to see the etiquette teacher talking with another girl.

How did I know she was the teacher? Keen observation and logical deduction. Plus, there was that picture of her from the website. (A thorough discussion of her name is coming up, but for now I will call her Mrs. Green.) I didn't know who the other girl was, but as she looked like a teenager, I assumed she was a fellow camper.

Green looked about 40. She had long blonde hair and was wearing a floral print dress. Tall and proud, she seemed out of place here at hillbilly heaven, like an ancient Greek statue in the National Cowgirl Museum in Fort Worth.

My mom ordered us outside to say hello.

Katie and I awkwardly walked up to her, and Mom ventured, "Mrs. Green?" to get her attention and introduce us.

Mrs. Green turned to greet us, her head held high, and said, "Why, hello." It was one of those "Why, hellos" that doesn't mean "Why, hello" at all, but rather, "What small creature shall I dismantle today?" She was like one of those vultures you see in cartoons with the big eyes and maliciously twisted grins. Remembering what vultures do to small creatures, my first instinct was to run, which I would have done if my mom hadn't been clutching my arm, already anticipating my move.

I decided to wait and watch because of Rule #1: Always wait for the enemy to make the first move. (I made up this rule.)

Mrs. Green fixed her penetrating gaze on me. "Oh, hello, Rachel, how are you? You're going to have so much fun this week. *MUAHAHAHAHA!!!*"

She didn't really say the last bit, but I knew she was thinking it.

Then she turned to Katie and said, "Hello, Katie. It's so nice to have you here."

Of course, she *would* be nicer to Katie.

23

That is your formal introduction to my antagonist—charming and debonair, but obviously dangerous. She was smiling, but I knew she was ready at any moment to bare her fangs of disdain at my lack of poise and puncture my vulnerable, unmannered skin. Like a vampire, she intended to poison my blood and turn me into a creature of austere etiquette rules and regulations!!!

When Mrs. Green said, "Why don't you come to the main room where the rest of the young ladies are waiting," I could see right through her. She did *not* think we were ladies. She thought we were rough and coarse and unworthy. I could feel her cold glare on me, those pupils swimming with reproach and contempt. I knew she was analyzing, judging and critiquing my salutation, my posture and my existence. My very SOUL!

Of course, my mom didn't notice anything of the sort (she never does) and did not heed my warnings about leaving me there for a week as we walked to the conference room in the main building. Grown-ups never listen and kids always have to take matters into their own hands to keep evil vampires/principals/etiquette teachers from taking over the WORLD!!!

With a heavy heart I made my way into the meeting room where the other girls and moms were waiting for the orientation to begin. We sat in the back and I began my customary scanning of the assembled to see which of my fellow campers I could make fun of first.

There were six girls besides Katie and me.

One was a fairly tall and pretty redhead from Tampa, Florida, who had a scar on her cheek that looked like a dimple. You know, redheads aren't technically *red* heads, they're orange heads, but we don't call them that because it sounds like an insult. She was wearing a striped hoodie and a floral skirt, so I assumed she was either artistic or crazy. I'll call her Evelyn, that's a pretty artistic name. She also had fake eyeglasses she would sometimes wear, which was…also artistic.

The girl beside her was African-American, of average height, and very athletic and sporty-looking; I'll dub her Asia—Asia from Atlanta. I later found out that she was a lifeguard, but she didn't exactly look like anybody I had seen on "Baywatch." That show is *so* misleading. Truth in advertising, people! Truth in advertising!

Next were Erica and Maggie, who were cousins like Katie and me, and also from Texas—what a small world. Their personalities were both like Katie's: loud and louder. Erica was heavier with short brown hair and Maggie was blonde and very tan from being a lifeguard. What are the odds? Two lifeguards at the same etiquette camp. The summer job of choice for teenagers, I guess.

Then there was Noelle, who turned out to be the nicest person on the planet. Brunette and of average height, she was from Michigan and pronounced her O's like A's (mam instead of mom, sacks instead of socks, etc.), but the darnedest, sweetest gal alive. She was always complimenting and helping everyone, and try as I might, I couldn't help but like her.

The odd woman out (besides myself) was Margaret. She was unusually tall, brunette, a philosophy major from a university in southern California—and 30 years old!

"Hm," I thought, "why would she willingly come to an etiquette camp with a bunch of pubescent teenagers? Perhaps she's at the wrong camp?" I knew *I* was.

By the way, I have assigned each girl a fake name to "protect their privacy" (i.e., so they won't sue me).

Which brings me to Mrs. Green.

As I mentioned, that was not our teacher's real name. It was actually something quite regal sounding, which was perfect for her because she was tall, majestic, and our sovereign for that week. What can I call her? Mrs. Queen? How about Pharaoh? Or Mrs. Hammurabi, since her word at camp was the supreme law of the land? That doesn't quite work. How about something Russian? Mrs. Roman-off? Maybe that's it. I googled Russian last names and found Alek-sashkin, but that seems awkward. I got it! Davenport! That sounds regal and sovereign. OK, she shall no longer be called Green, but Davenport evermore.

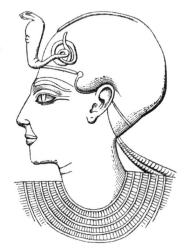

So, you've now met Davenport and my campmates.

Usually, the worst part about meeting people is the uncomfortable introductory conversation where everyone pretends to be nicer than they actually are and acts like they care what school you go to and if you like it there. So, I always tune people out during introductions. As a result, I can't remember any actual conversation that took place at that moment—all I remember is my own inner monologue, which can be summarized in two words: *Why me?* But, I can improvise some of that initial conversation for your edification.

Evelyn: *Salutations, comrade! How dost thou fareth?*

Asia: *Like, well. Twas like good fortune that allows my presence.*

Evelyn: *Hark, do I hear a footfall?*

Erica: *It is I, Don Juan!*

Davenport: *I am Pharaoh! I am the morning and the evening star! My teachings are sacrament and shall be branded onto thine backs so thou shalt not ever forget them!*

Katie: *BLAHBLAHBLAHalsdkfjaweoriuasØæþÿëîúùð=* *

I was miserable. I didn't want to be there, and I certainly didn't want to spend seven days with these people. I was ready to leave NOW. In fact, I was planning the perfect escape in my mind: I would pack my suitcase before dinner and hide my room key under the cow skull next to the door. I would need some sort of getaway vehicle, and since Mom's was not an option, my sister Sarah would come to my rescue in a red Bugatti, sneaking my suitcase out of my room (using the key surreptitiously hidden under the cow skull) into the trunk of the car. Then, at exactly 7:01, I would dash out of the dining hall, away from all those perky people, hop into the car and get whisked away to sweet freedom! No wait—I would give a triumphant laugh first, and shout, "So long, SUCKERS!" as I ditched Katie, my hair waving in the wind behind me.

I couldn't realistically implement the plan, though, mainly because I didn't have long hair. If it weren't for that, I would have been *so* out of there. Instead, despite my desperate final pleas to take me with her, my mom abandoned me to my fate. She didn't glance back even once as she drove off in a cloud of Paradise dust.

CHAPTER 3

HURRICANE RACHEL

Our first session began that same day in the main meeting room of the hotel. The room was very large and the decor old-time Texas-style, like the rest of the resort. The classroom part had walls made of wooden logs. Long tables for us to sit at formed a sort of U in front of Davenport's desk. There was a white dry erase board off to the side behind her and two other paper boards next to it. In back, there was a table for iced tea and water. Conspicuously missing was a clock.

I note the clock thing because that is the most important part of any classroom—it tells me how much longer I have to endure whatever it is I'm doing.

Katie and I sat at the back table.

Davenport made sure to cast an intimidating glance over the room before she began, "Everything you will learn here is related to having respect for yourself and others. How you present yourself to the world is just one aspect of that."

I could see where this was going. Just picture me making the same face as when I'm eating a lime.

"Different situations call for different attire and attitude." She warmed to her subject. "One type of attire is not appropriate for every situation. Sometimes it is appropriate to be in a suit, sometimes it is appropriate to be in a bikini, and sometimes it is even appropriate to be naked."

Noelle got all flustered at the word "naked" and spilled her iced tea all over Erica's shorts. Perfect timing. There was a little scuffle while Noelle got some napkins and we all made weird faces about the naked comment. What was she talking about, nude beaches?

Davenport continued unperturbed, "What I meant by that was, it is appropriate to be naked in the bath and shower."

Lame-o! We were looking for intrigue!

She then began to explain the importance of making a good first impression. She told us that it is essential to have proper clothing and posture and hair—they are all vital to making a good first impression. She said that people will have a specific reaction to us depending on what we initially say, how we're dressed and the body language we convey.

So, whenever I meet somebody new, I needed to remember to stand up straight, be dressed appropriately and respectfully, have combed my hair, and smile and say hello. That's a lot to manage all at once. I wondered if it was enough if I just brushed my teeth.

To illustrate her point, Davenport had us do an exercise. "Now girls," she said, "turn to the first section in your binders titled 'The Importance of First Impressions.' We're going to play a little game to see what our first impressions of each other are. In the pocket of your binder do you see a little sheet with the words 'weather, color, car…' on it? Yes, that's it. Now write your name at the top, and I want you to pass the sheets around so each person can put down a word that fits each category for you. Fill out what kind of color, weather, music and car you thought of when you first met each of the other girls."

When I got my results back, they read:

1. **Color:** Orange, White, Black, Brown, Red, Yellow, Red.
2. **Weather:** Humid, Winter, Winter, Spring, Hurricane, Summer, Fall.
3. **Music:** Rock, Pop, Pop, Alternative, Classical, Alternative, Hip-hop.
4. **Car:** Luxury car, Car, Hummer, Sports Car, Buggy, Truck, Sports Car.

I scrutinized them, wondering if I should take them as lame attempts at not offending me, or as actual analogies of the aura I gave off. The colors were pretty much on target, but humid? Was that a hit about the state of my hair? And hurricane?? Did I look violent and intent on wiping out New Orleans? Maybe it was my new bangs; they *were* sort of edgy. I have to admit, though, the music was dead on. The girl who wrote luxury car actually spelled it "lugery car," and the girl who wrote "car" on my sheet, well, that was very insightful of her, now wasn't it?

None of us could fill out a card for Davenport. Yes, I asked. And was flatly refused. Perhaps it was because she didn't want to be judged like the rest of us, or didn't want to have to go through the pain of deciphering every abstruse one-word clue about her, like "lugery."

Meanwhile, she soldiered on about body language. "Did you know, girls, that it only takes 10 seconds for someone to figure out what they think of you? And if it's a bad first impression, the damage that's done could take years to fix. People take their initial reaction to you more seriously than any of your subsequent actions."

I must have a lot of enemies right now.

Then, out of nowhere we heard a loud smacking sound on the left side of the room. We all turned to see Erica happily popping her pink bubble gum. Davenport became strangely quiet. She looked down on Erica with a stare so chilly it would make ice shudder. She didn't say anything...didn't have to. Erica all but shriveled in front of her and meekly placed her bubble gum on a paper napkin.

We learned then that the silent wrath of Davenport, piercing and intense, was worse than any possible yelling she could have done.

Mercifully, that was the end of it. She dismissed us by solemnly intoning, "Remember, the initial impression you make could change the course of your lives."

A bit melodramatic, don't you think? But I guess she had to say something over the top for us to contemplate the seriousness of that lesson.

So, we all went out to explore the resort. Some of the girls suggested we go swimming to get to know each other, and Katie and I went to go get our bathing suits. By then it was already dark, and for some reason I always associate late-night swims with skinny-dipping, so I was a little apprehensive since there were several girls there I would rather not see in their birthday suits (they didn't have the greatest figures). Thankfully, none of that happened, and we just sat around the hot tub discussing where we were from, what our parents did, and how it was so perfect that Noelle spilled her tea when Davenport said "naked."

The only one missing from our little group was Margaret. During the rest of the week, I noticed that she didn't hang out with us much. I assumed it was because she was so much older than the rest of us. I actually don't know what she did the whole time we weren't in class. I imagined she was probably planning world domination. Or more accurately, thinking of the philosophy behind world domination.

Everyone else seemed so excited about the next day, I figured things might be looking up, and so I decided to postpone my escape. Maybe Davenport would come up with some more awkward comments that would make my day. In any case, I fell asleep about 10 p.m., hopeful and optimistically pessimistic.

CHAPTER 4

WHEN A STRANGER CALLS

Waking up suddenly from a deep sleep is akin to being barked at in the face by a yipping Chihuahua. It's jolting, unpleasant, makes your eyes squint, and makes you want to hit the Chihuahua in the face.

I came up with that analogy after the front desk rang the room at the crack of dawn the next morning. According to the schedule, we had to be at breakfast by 8 a.m., so for some reason I had asked for a wake-up call at 6:45 a.m. I would never make *that* mistake again.

If I sleep well on the first night away from home, I have no idea where I am in the morning. So I groped around frantically for the source of the racket, thinking, "What the heck?" I finally picked up the receiver with a "You-hi-what are we-*hello?*" The lady on the other end laughed and said something like, "It's time to get up." In my mind I thought I had said, "Thank you, bye." But later Katie told me that I just grunted and hung up the phone. By then I had remembered where I was and why Katie was with me, and I have to admit that I was somewhat (and inexplicably) excited about the day. It was a point of weakness of my naïve, impressionable mind!

Day 2 of our lessons began with what Davenport called "electronic etiquette," a highfalutin way of saying "telephone manners." Frankly, I hate the telephone because I never really understand what the other person is saying, so I try to avoid that experience altogether, if I can.

But actually, I was looking forward with amusement to Davenport teaching telephone etiquette, because right before my trip to camp, I had had a painful experience with someone else's phone manners. I rang one of my teachers at home—let's call her Mrs. Patterson—and her 18-year-old daughter answered in a saccharine, super sweet, syrupy Southern voice. "Hellllllllooooo?"

"Hi, this is Rachel, may I please speak to Mrs. Patterson?"

"Yes, you may," she purred. "One moment, pullleezz!" This, said very breathily.

Then she put down the phone, and SCREAMED in the loudest humanly possible voice: "MMMMMMOOMMMMM!!!!!! TELLLEPHONE!!!!!!!!!!!!!!!!!!"

I'm still traumatized.

So, like I said, I had a reason to be happy that this topic would be covered.

Here then, are the rules for how *not* to be rude on the phone:

> ❁ **You have to speak clearly and loudly enough to be heard.** (But not too loudly—refer to story above: my ears are still ringing!)
>
> ❁ **Do not eat, drink or chew gum when you are speaking to someone on the phone.** (That sounds like a no-brainer, but I bet a bunch of people do it.)

> ✿ If you are calling someone's house, you shouldn't call too early or too late in the day.
> ✿ You should also ask if this is a good time to talk.
> ✿ You shouldn't stay on the phone too long.

I wanted to show my sister this list since it contradicted the sheer essence of her female teenagehood, e.g., don't stay on the phone for a long time, avoid doing other activities when calling—hah! Come to think of it, that guy in "When a Stranger Calls" broke almost every rule on this list. He didn't even ask Camilla Belle if it was a good time to talk! Geez.

Davenport also told us we should identify ourselves when we call someone. We should say something like, "Hello, Mrs. Jones. This is Rachel. May I please speak to Melissa?"

That got me thinking. My mom taught me to always say my name whenever I answer the phone at our house, so I always say, "Hello, this is Rachel."

When I asked Davenport if that was permissible, she said no because it was giving the caller, who could be a stranger, a window into my life, and he could come find me and…and…steal my puppies. Instead, if someone calls your home, you should just say "hello," and when they ask to speak to your mom or dad, you should say, "Yes, you may. One moment, please."

I wish I had known that the last time my mom's attorney called our house. Here's how that went.

Me: *Hello, this is Rachel.* (Gasp! Window into my soul!)
Attorney: *Hi Rachel, this is Grant. Can I talk to your mom?*

Me: *No.*

Click.

My mom is still mad at me.

Then Davenport turned the discussion to cell phones and other mobile devices.

Apparently, land lines and cellular phones have two different sets of etiquette rules, as if one wasn't enough.

But actually, they all seemed pretty reasonable once I heard them. If we all used them, there would be a lot fewer car accidents and people falling down open manholes and stuff.

- ❀ **When you call someone on their cell phone, don't talk too long because some people pay by the minute.**

- ❀ **Never talk while driving.**

- ❀ **There are many places where we should NOT take our cell phones. They include: restaurants, stores, movie theaters, churches, schools, restrooms and any other public area. It just is not appropriate to carry on a conversation in public.**

- ❀ **When you are using a cell phone—to text or talk— in the presence of another person, you are essentially saying that there is someone else more important to you than the person you're with. And that is just plain rude.** (Cough, cough, sister Sarah.)

- ❀ **Texting while driving is an absolute no-no! Very, very dangerous!**

So, basically, the cell phone is virtually useless since it cannot be used in any public arena, vehicle, or in the presence of anyone else. Listening to Davenport, I guess one would have to conclude that cell phones must have been invented for the hermits of this world.

CHAPTER 5

SCARY SILVERWARE

After that session, it was time for lunch. This was our first official meal together. We made our way to the dining hall, meeting Erica and Maggie on the way. Davenport was already seated at the head of the table with an imperial air (of course). We took our places and waited for the others to arrive since we couldn't start eating until everyone was there. As the waitress set a plate of grilled chicken, rice and fresh vegetables down before me, Davenport informed us that all of our meals would be plated—she actually said that, rather than "formal," even though "plated" literally means "covered with a layer of metal." We had two, tasty three-course meals a day with two snacks in between. For breakfast we were on our own.

Of course, I didn't eat all that was offered because, after having recently read "The Silver Chair," I suspected they were stuffing us for the purpose of slaughtering and eating us at the end of the week.

Davenport informed us that every meal would be a practice session for our dining etiquette skills. That basically meant no rest for the weary (and hungry).

We Americans always find a way of improving something that was perfectly fine to begin with and overcomplicating it in the process. After rejecting the metric system and the Celsius scale of temperature (in favor of inches, feet, yards and degrees of Fahrenheit), they tackled table etiquette. The simple and practical European way of eating is to keep utensils in the same hands throughout the meal—fork in the left hand, knife in the right—while the American way is to cut, put down the knife, switch the fork to the other hand and eat. Then, switch back and repeat for the next bite, and so on.

Davenport, bless her heart, focused on the European way of holding our knife and fork. We had to sit rigidly upright and weren't allowed to turn over our forks to spear and scoop up our food like every other person in the United States (except for soft stuff like rice and mashed potatoes). That's right, it's not proper etiquette. You have to hold the fork with the arch up and just put whatever food you can't pin down onto the back. It was

almost impossible, so for every meal thereafter, I would wait until Davenport wasn't looking and then quickly shovel food onto my fork and inhale.

There were a lot of miniscule rules that I don't think I will ever fully grasp. Apparently, wars have been started over little things like the placement of eating utensils and seating arrangements.

On one occasion I was sitting next to Katie at the table, talking with Evelyn, when all of a sudden I heard:

D: *Rachel, Katie feels threatened right now.*

Me: *Huh? I mean, excuse me?*

I looked over at Katie, thinking that maybe she sensed an aura of menace on my part, but she looked just as confused as I felt. I asked Davenport what she was talking about, but, sphinx-like, she wasn't offering any clues.

D: *She still feels threatened.*

Me: *I'll protect you Katie! Don't be scared!*

The other girls laughed. Davenport didn't even crack a smile.

D (icy): *The blade of your knife is facing her!*

Me: *What?*

I looked at the knife lying next to my plate. The blade was indeed facing Katie instead of toward the plate. The thought that Katie felt threatened by a knife resting two feet away from her on the table was so ridiculous that I couldn't help gaping sardonically at Davenport—the only time I didn't try to hide my total disdain at the absurdity of some of these rules. But she wasn't intimidated. She willfully ignored me as if she had already anticipated my reaction.

Not only were there weird knife rules, but we also had to follow strict guidelines for passing food dishes.

> ❀ You may pass dishes to the right only.
> ❀ You may not hand items across the table, but must pass them the long way round.

I wasn't the only one who would wait until Davenport wasn't looking to secretly pass sauces to the person sitting across from me.

While we were making sure our table companions did not feel threatened, we also had to use the dining times as an opportunity for each girl to tell about herself. The first to break the ice was Erica, and she decided to talk about her horses and puppies and rabbits and other cute farm animals. Asia and Maggie talked about lifeguarding and tan lines. Mine was pretty much me looking at Katie for suggestions of what to say.

When it came time for the afternoon session, Davenport announced we were going to have a guest instructor who would teach us all about nutrition. It wasn't enough to learn how to eat, now we had to learn *what* to eat as well. Yipeee!

CHAPTER 6

YOU ARE WHAT YOU EAT

I thought it a bit ironic that we would have a nutrition specialist talk to us after all the food they stuffed us with.

When I saw the diet lady through the window, waddling down the boardwalk to the conference room, my first thought was, "*She's* teaching us nutrition?" I thought she was a little on the heavyset side, but she later told us that she used to weigh 200 pounds, and now she was only about 150, so I guess she was looking pretty good.

By the way, her name was Kalinda (not really).

She lined up a variety of soda pops and packaged yummy-looking but fattening goodies on the table from which Davenport usually preached, and spoke to us about how unhealthy soft drinks and cookies and chips are.

I know she's right, but it seems that no matter how many times I hear warnings about the horrible side effects of soda and processed food, my biased memory disposes of the information in a few days, and I just go back to indulging in them. For instance, even though Kalinda told us that the dye used to make strawberry-flavored yogurt comes from the bodies of crushed beetles (seriously), I continue to eat and enjoy it.

According to Kalinda, proper nutrition requires that we:

✿ **Drink water every day.**

✿ **Eat lean protein foods, such as turkey and fish.**

✿ **Consume lots of fruits, vegetables, whole grains, and low-fat dairy, such as milk, cheese and yogurt.**

✿ **Watch our portions.** Apparently, they should only be the size of the outstretched palm of your hand.

✿ **Exercise regularly and avoid stress.**

That's all well and good but, according to Kalinda, everything that's sold in grocery stores is unhealthy because the meat is infused with carbon dioxide to make it look happy and the fruit and vegetables have chemicals added to make them look shiny and fresh. I believe it, but what else are we supposed to do? I guess I could try slaughtering my own cows. Maybe take up farming as well, abandon my dreams of becoming a writer or going to medical school. I'm sure my dad won't mind.

After Kalinda left, we had…dinner! Apparently, her lecture didn't make much of an impact on the others either, because everybody helped themselves to the beetle-infested strawberry yogurt. Ewwwwwwww.

We went to our rooms, stuffed and exhausted. Katie had, like, 500 texts. I had none. All her texts concerned Logan and Samantha and all her friends who were being mean to her for no apparent reason, and she felt the need to dive thoroughly into each topic while I practiced my selective hearing.

I figured it was my turn for once, and so on this day I told Katie this story: "A really long time ago, like when I was eight or something, my dad told me about a man who had two wives, one who was older than he was and one who was younger. Every day the older wife would pluck out her husband's brown hairs so people wouldn't think she married a younger man, and every day the younger wife would pluck out his gray hairs so people wouldn't think she married an older man until, eventually, the man was bald."

For some reason my story made me laugh so hard, I shook uncontrollably on the floor with tears rolling down my eyes...until I noticed that Katie wasn't paying attention to anything I said.

"Katie, are you even listening?"

"Hmm? Yeah, ha-ha, that's funny. Hey, Lauren just texted me after she told me to stop talking to her...."

I was left wondering why she wasn't listening to my story about the bald man with two wives. Was she offended by the polygamy theme? Or was it just not that interesting of a story? Even if she didn't think it was, *I* had to listen to her 1001 stories about Logan, so she could at least pay attention to *one* of mine.

This was when I started to get a little dubious about her listening skills. If it was hard for Katie to sit through my one little tiny story (83 words, to be exact), which was considerably shorter than the Gettysburg Address (278 words, to be exact), then how would she fare with the Listening Skills section of her school's standardized test? Huh? Answer me that!

CHAPTER 7

ATTENTION!

During the next day's morning session, we learned all about proper handshakes and posture.

Apparently, it's good manners to always shake hands with whomever you have just met, man or woman. "Smile warmly and sincerely," Davenport counseled, "establish eye contact, establish a face-to-face stance, bring your hand up your side with your thumb pointed to the ceiling, and establish a firm and complete grasp, both palms in full contact. Shake from your elbow. Two to four pumps are sufficient. Be aware of fragrance on your hands, hold beverages in your left hand so your right hand is free, and think about the handshake you are giving and receiving." All together now.

There were also a lot of handshake "don'ts." Avoid the following:

> ❀ Keeping a space between your palms; it means you have something to hide.
>
> ❀ The LINGERING HANDSHAKE, when you keep it going for more than four pumps.

> ✿ The SHAKY HANDSHAKE, when you shake from your shoulder up.
>
> ✿ The PULSE-TAKER, when you tap your forefinger to the other person's palm like you're checking their pulse.
>
> ✿ The LIMP HANDSHAKE (also known as the DEAD FISH HANDSHAKE), when you don't have a firm grip.
>
> ✿ The VISE SQUEEZE (or the "I'M A REAL MAN HANDSHAKE"), when you grasp too tightly.

I wished that some of my parents' male business partners were around to hear this lesson, because I can't tell you how many times I've had to see a physical therapist after one of them had almost crushed the bones in my hand.

When I realized that I was guilty of the lingering handshake, tending to hold on for the duration of the introduction, I decided to mend my ways. My new strategy is to "get in and get out," so I don't look needy.

Davenport taught us one additional lesson—the handy-dandy hug-block, which is the extremely obvious way of telling someone you don't want their germs all over you. Here's how it works:

Enter gross, unappealing (possibly sweaty) character. As he approaches, you go through the following five steps:

1. **Look disgusted.**

2. **Completely extend hand directly in front of you.**

3. **Take step back with left foot and place right foot forward in line with extended hand.**

4. Watch in pleasure as the gross, unappealing (possibly sweaty) character is thwarted from getting his equally gross, unappealing (possibly sweaty) germs all over you.

5. Laugh maliciously.

I added the first, fourth and fifth steps. I have to admit, though, that Davenport was dead-on with the other two.

Next, we had posture lessons, which if I recall correctly, were definitely one of the punishments in Dante's circles of hell, probably the ones punishing the slothful and wrathful.

Davenport seemed extra excited about the posture lesson. "Okay ladies," she instructed, "stand with your feet about two inches from the wall…have the back of your head touch it…and pull your pelvis in—that's the most important part—so you don't look like you're sticking your chest out. Make sure there's just a hand's space between your back and the wall…"

It felt like stretching your back muscles and toning your hips. Sitting down was twice as excruciating, and since you couldn't tuck your pelvis in, it made you stick out your boobs like you wanted someone to look at your chest. It's misery when you experience agony while in what's supposed to be a relaxing position.

Then Davenport made us walk up and down the room to evaluate our poise. We couldn't be rigid-legged or let our arms swing (oh, by the way, you're not supposed to swing your arms when you walk) or place our feet down the wrong way (it's heel first, then sole). Doing the whole I'm-the-queen-of-the-world strut was almost as annoying as those itchy pantyhose you had to wear when you were little. *Ooooh,* I hated those! When I have my own daughter, I will never make her wear pantyhose.

Asia was the best at the posture lessons. I think it's because she had good calves. I, of course, was never able to get my walk up to Davenport's standards. Each time I lumbered across the room, she found something wrong. I thought it terribly unfair when she imitated what I was doing because she grossly exaggerated the faults.

"No, Rachel, you can't extend your hand like *this;* you need to do it like *this.*"

"That's what I just did!"

"No, you did it like *this,* not like *this.*"

Sigh.

It was sort of like when my flute teacher says to me, "No, you're supposed to keep your mouth wide and keep your tongue down at this part!"

And I say, "That's what I was doing."

And she says, "No, *this* is what you were doing," and then proceeds to make spitting and sputtering noises with her flute in imitation of me. It was just like that, except Davenport didn't spit and sputter.

Next, we learned how to turn the proper way.

When you're walking and ready to turn, you put your right heel two inches away from your left toes, and without moving your feet, twist your body around until you're facing the other way. If these instructions are getting lost in translation, let me put it this way: just look like you desperately need to use the restroom.

Finally, it was time to learn how to bend down and pick up an object in a ladylike manner.

"Does anyone know how to pick something up properly?" Davenport asked.

All of us simultaneously yelled, "You beeeeend, then snap!"—a "Legally Blonde" reference.

If you haven't seen "Legally Blonde," you are but half a woman.

Davenport laughed, but I'm sure she had no idea what we were talking about, since she didn't seem like the kind of person who watches movies.

She continued, "If you just bend at the hips like almost everybody does, then you have your behind stuck out and it's kind of awkward, right? So, to pick something up properly, you need to have one foot slightly in front of the other, and then bend at the knees and pick it up with one hand."

She proceeded to demonstrate for us, first warning that her knees always crack when she does it. Good to know. Her knees *did* crack, but she did it perfectly anyway. Of course.

It's as easy as it sounds, except for the part about keeping your balance and not rolling over like Humpty Dumpty when you bend

down. No matter how hard I tried, I could not master it and did it incorrectly every time, repeatedly earning Davenport's haughty scorn.

When class was over, Katie and I walked up and down the halls doing the cool turn in synchrony.

Then it was time for lunch. I'd be willing to give the details if I could, but I don't have the slightest

recollection of anything anyone said since it was another round of the most exceedingly boring prattle about dogs and hobbies, blah, blah,

blah, blah. I just drowned out the noise with the good food, for once not caring if it all accumulated as fat.

CHAPTER 8

TEA, ANYONE?

That afternoon Davenport discussed the importance of writing Thank You notes.

"With the invention of email," she lamented, "Thank You notes have become a lost art."

She went on to say that this was no excuse not to send one when the occasion warranted, as when someone sent you a gift, or did something nice for you, or remembered you in a kind way.

Davenport insisted that Thank You notes must meet the five following criteria:

> ✿ Be sent within three to five days of receiving the thing you're thankful for.
>
> ✿ Look neat and be grammatically correct.
>
> ✿ Reference specifically what you are thankful for.
>
> ✿ Mention how you are using the gift.
>
> ✿ Include a personal comment about yourself.

Then she made us practice by writing at least 12 dozen Thank You notes—one to every person who taught, served or so much as looked at us at camp, including the dietitian, our waitresses and the chef. I ran out of ideas about how to make them personal after eight cards—which was more than the others put together wrote (smug grin).

By the time we finished and moved on to tea etiquette lessons, my hand was about to fall off.

The tea manners Davenport taught were as posh and pretentious as "high tea" looks in those "Masterpiece Theater" dramas about Merry Olde England. Davenport went on at excruciating length about proper tea time, proper placement of plates and cups, and proper ways of pouring tea.

I wish I could tell you the rules but, frankly, I wasn't listening, because, unless you live in Great Britain, this is not essential information to a teenager. The only thing I remember is that you're not actually supposed to stick your pinky up when you drink tea.

"It's too pretentious," Davenport said. "Would you stick your pinky up if you were drinking a glass of water? No. So don't do it when you drink tea, either."

Yes, ma'am.

After the tea lesson and another filling meal, we all sat around and talked. Katie was jabbering on about some nonsense, but Noelle looked enthralled, as if Katie were telling how she was next in line to the throne of Candy Land or something. Noelle was the kind of person who expressed an interest in everything you said. She always smiled and nodded when you talked, making you feel like the most important person in the room. It was a wonderful characteristic to have, and it made everyone love her. I thought about this as I watched Noelle interact with Katie and wondered how she had acquired that ability. I secretly wished I could do that.

Anyway, Noelle and Katie talked late into the night while I listened, and we didn't go to bed until the wee hours of the morning.

CHAPTER 9

THIS WON'T HURT A BIT...

The next morning in class, I was still half asleep when Davenport thundered, "Nails!!"

"Hmmm, what?"

Katie shook me and pointed to the section in our folders marked "Nail Care." Apparently it had something to do with how to paint our nails. At that moment, I realized I had not brought my bottle of nail polish to camp with me. I was quite upset about it. Really. That might sound melodramatic, except it didn't feel that way at the time. I couldn't touch up my nails with the color I had on. It's very irritating to have chipped nail polish and no way to fix it.

Actually, that does happen to some people, and they don't care—they get gross chips and randomly decide to peel the polish off their fingernails and onto their desk that is right by yours, so you're left to stare in disgust at the shavings falling five inches away from your arm—gross!

I'm not making this part up. My otherwise perfect sister does it ALL THE TIME! I'm always finding nail polish shavings all over her things. Not only that; they're SPARKLY nail polish shavings to go along with the sparkly pink fairies and sparkly pink unicorns all over her room—remnants from the days she fantasized about being a fairy princess. That's OK if you're three years old, but when you're 18, please!

Anyway, here's the 411 regarding nails and nail care: According to Davenport, after the face, nails are the second thing that people notice about us. So, we should take the time to have properly manicured nails. She said that 75% of employers polled agree that neatly manicured nails will increase a potential applicant's chances of getting hired.

Some tips for proper nail care include:

> ❀ Filing your nails in only one direction (like an oval shape).
> ❀ Don't cut them too short.
> ❀ Or let them grow too long.
> ❀ And—yes!—don't leave your nail polish with chips in it.

You should always touch up the nail polish if it has peeled or chipped off. Take note, Sarah.

To illustrate all this, Davenport said we were going to have a proper manicure. She brought out a big pot of boiling wax, which we all took turns sticking our fingers into while trying not to cry. Seriously, it was freaking HOT! My mom won't let me use the word "freaking," but no other word works here that isn't worse, so I'm going to risk it. Supposedly, the wax locks moisture into your hands. Anybody ever heard of *hand lotion* as an alternative to searing hot beeswax?

I looked at the instructions for properly manicuring nails:

> ✿ Soak in warm water.
> ✿ Push back cuticles.
> ✿ Buff and polish with a base and top coat.

Needless to say, I had no idea what buffing was (still don't), and I didn't know why I needed a base coat and a top coat if she wasn't going to let us paint watermelons and palm trees on our toenails. Apparently, designs are a big no-no, which is a blow to "Toe-rrific," the only beauty-related book I've ever purchased. Look it up at *www.toerrific.com.* It's the bomb.

CHAPTER 10

DIAMOND HEAD

Before we began our afternoon lecture on makeup, Davenport told everyone they should know the shape of their head. She stalked around the room to evaluate each girl. She labeled the other girls triangle, inverted triangle, heart, square and octagon (just kidding), but when she came up to me, she pulled back my hair and uttered, "Hmmm… I'd say diamond."

"Diamond…?"

"Yes, your head is diamond-shaped."

Diamond-shaped? I have a long face with a pointy chin and forehead and pokey cheeks?! Is that what I look like?!?

Sensational!

I gazed at her, outraged. The steam that must have come from my ears probably accentuated the diamond angles.

Unfazed, Davenport continued and said that the shape of your head determines the manner in which you should apply your makeup. As you can imagine, I *love* makeup and wear it *every* day, and it takes me *hours* to put it on and I just *love* the way I look in it. Not!

Davenport sent us to our rooms for the makeup we brought with us to camp. I returned with the single item in my "kit"—a tube of concealer. It was weird concealer at that—half of it green and the other half beige—and I didn't really know how to use it. What was the green part of the tube for? Why would I put green on my blemishes? A little conspicuous, don't cha think?

I felt a bit silly when I saw Maggie's 12 x 12 makeup box, but that was nothing compared to when Davenport's razor sharp glare hit me squarely between the eyes. I had disappointed her yet again, and her eyes narrowed as if to say, "You've got a long way to go, girlfriend."

Just when I thought I might escape unscathed, Davenport brought in a basketful of makeup and a set of magnifying mirrors for us to use. Seeing all that makeup made me grumpy. What's the point of putting eyeliner on your waterline? Isn't that dangerous? How do you not poke your eyes out? Plus, you never realize how ugly you actually are until you look at your skin magnified 12 times. Eeek!

As intriguing as Davenport tried to make it sound, I tuned out after about 11 seconds. When the girls started to do each other's makeup, I sat down on my swivel chair and began twirling around. Things that normally make others happy, such as shopping and makeup and hanging out talking about their six-inch heels, make me cranky. Go figure.

Davenport noticed my studied disinterest and said I could leave early. Yeeeessss—score!!!!

I skipped back to my room and read until dinner. Afterward, once again stuffed, I sat around and finished my book while the other girls walked around the compound exploring.

Later I called my mom to complain that it was 11 p.m. and I was still awake.

She said, "Go to sleep, then."

CHAPTER 11

TOE CLEAVAGE

The next day, Davenport wanted to teach us about wearing proper attire. Yay! Yet another thing to make me feel inadequate. I turned to the page in the manual marked "Wardrobe Building" to discuss professional outfits and wardrobe do's and don'ts.

Davenport began by saying that what we wear communicates a lot about us.

✿ V-necks in sweaters communicate authority.

✿ A third garment like a jacket or blazer conveys confidence and authority as well.

✿ Don't wear big and clanky jewelry; it's loud and distracting.

✿ Don't let your unmentionables show under your clothes—like bra straps or panty lines.

✿ If you wear a blouse with a collar to a job interview, it looks more professional.

✿ Pantyhose is a must.

✿ Toe cleavage at work is a no-no.

Toe cleavage—that's a new one.

Davenport continued sternly, "I said everything we learn here would be related to respect for self and others, including your wardrobe; so I want to discuss with you a very sensitive matter— what you wear in front of men. I think all you girls know what men think about when they see a scantily clad young woman."

Why in the name of heaven is she talking about this??

"Men are very visual, and when we, as women, show as much skin as we do…"

Lalalalalalalalalalalala. I don't hear you!!!!!

She insisted on opening this topic up for discussion, so everyone could have their little input.

If there is one topic I hate talking about, it's anything sexually suggestive. It makes me uncomfortable and nervous, and I don't want to hear anything about it. Ever! My fellow campmates, on the other hand, didn't seem the least bothered by this turn of conversation.

Maggie: *Oh, I know they just think about it all the time.*

Me: *Jingle bells, jingle bells, jingle all the way…*

Katie: *Oh yeah, the girls at my school dress like sluts, so no wonder the guys are—*

Me: *Oh, what fun it is to ride in a one horse open sleeeiiigh…*

Erica: *I mean, puh-leeze, something for the imagination!*

Me: *Dashing through the airport…*

Davenport: *And also, ladies, not only do we need to be careful in the way we dress, but also in the way we interact with boys.*

Me: *in a one horse open marshmallows roasting on an open fire...*

Davenport: *When we hug boys, we tend to hug them full on...*

Me: *Laughing all the waaaaay; Frosty laughing and singing on a one horse open sleigh—is it safe yet?!?!*

Davenport: *So, instead, it's best to give them a side hug with one arm.*

Duly noted. Can this be over now?

But before dismissing us, Davenport said, "Remember, ladies, we have dance class tonight, so be ready by seven!"

I hardly heard her. I couldn't get out of there fast enough.

CHAPTER 12

SHALL WE DANCE?

We all had dinner together. Afterward I was resting on my bed, feeling tired and fat from the non-stop gorge fest that we had indulged in at dinner, while Katie was fixing her hair. Mine could've used washing, but I didn't really care. All we were going to do was learn ballroom dancing with what I presumed was some 60-year-old lady. Katie was blabbing on about Logan (I know, you're shocked), when I heard people walking by on the boardwalk and the sound of boys laughing.

I wondered who it was, since we were the only guests on this side of the hotel, but I thought nothing more of it and continued to nod off for another five minutes.

Suddenly, there was an urgent knock, and before I could answer it, Asia burst into our room. "Rachel! Katie! There are BOYS here to dance with us!!"

Katie flung her head around and I sat up on the bed.

What?!!?

"There are *boys* in *tuxedos* here to dance with us!"

"Oh my gosh, are you serious???!!!" I spluttered.

"No, I'm lying," Asia retorted indignantly.

Oh my gosh, there are BOYS here to dance with us!!!!!!!!!

I leapt from my bed and started throwing on proper attire, all the
while screaming, "Are you SERIOUS!!!???"

I had just assumed that we'd be dancing
with each other.

*Oh my gosh, there are BOYS here to
dance with us!!!!!!!!!*

I already said that, didn't I?

In case you're perplexed over my
reaction and the gravity of the situation, I'll

try to be as succinct as possible. I was *not* excited for the same reasons
the other girls *were* excited. I'm not boy crazy, in fact boys *make* me
crazy. But for the moment, all I could process was:

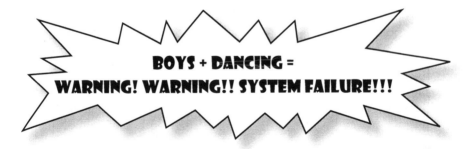

BOYS + DANCING =
WARNING! WARNING!! SYSTEM FAILURE!!!

That was flashing through my mind as I panicked about what to do
with my hair. I frantically tried to straighten it and feign the appearance
of a clean updo. I put on the shoes with heels that I'd brought along
(for visual poise), and Katie and I stepped outside.

We joined the rest of the girls peeping in through the windows
of the meeting room to get a look at our dance partners for the

evening. Contrary to Asia's report, they were *not* wearing tuxedos, but dress pants and button-down shirts with those fancy shiny shoes I'd seen my dad put on for special occasions. Obviously, the other girls saw things that I didn't, because the only thing I heard for the next five minutes was, "They are soooooo hot!" and other phrases with variations on that word.

Thirty-year-old Margaret's reaction was a little less enthusiastic. I chuckled inwardly at her look of "I can't believe they're making me do this."

Get in line, Margaret...get in line.

What occurred to me during all the loud giggling was that Davenport had failed to inform us about this little social gathering. I was furious, almost as furious as when she told me I had a diamond-shaped head.

Just then, she walked up and the girls all showered her with accolades for keeping the big surprise a secret. I didn't say anything and just glared—hoping she would notice.

She didn't.

When we went inside, there were seven boys standing around (which meant one of us would have to dance with the teacher). They looked very polite and eager to dance with us—six deluded teenage girls, one visibly uncomfortable older woman, and one oily-haired, panicking grouch.

"Katie, psst, Katie, how do I look?" I whispered anxiously.

"You look fine, why?"

"My hair isn't oily, and I don't look like I just woke up?"

"Uh, no, your hair isn't oily, it just looks shiny. You look great, Rachel."

"Okay, thanks."

I didn't know if it was just lip service (since she was really good at making you think you looked pretty when you didn't), but I hoped that the line between "shiny" and "oily" was clearly distinguishable.

As if on cue, the boys introduced themselves. There was Brandon, who had some skin issues; Justin, who looked like a wax figure; Dustin, who had braces; Thomas, who sported spiked hair, and Zim, who was the most cheerful creature I've seen since Elmo. I don't remember the other two very well.

The dance teacher's name was Melanie. She was blonde and tall, wore a pretty blue dress and had a funny smile, and seemed very nice—hard to believe since she was apparently a good friend of Davenport.

"All right, ladies," she cooed, "tonight we will be learning the basic steps of the waltz and the foxtrot."

I started rocking back on my heels and stealing quick glances at the boys, who were making fleeting, flirtatious eye contact with the other girls. (You know what I'm talking about; you've all done it.)

"Now, the first steps of the waltz are back with your right foot… left with your left foot…then forward, right, and back again." Melanie demonstrated the moves as she talked. "You'll want to count a beat to help you with this—**one**-two-three, **four**-five-six.…"

Some-body-*kill*-me-now.

Then Melanie had us do the steps holding our "imaginary partner" while the boys watched. I made sure to hold my hands up lackadaisically, so they'd know I wasn't feelin' it. Then we did the foxtrot—"slow, slow, quick, quick"—with the promenade, which was my favorite part of the dance.

We started our dancing rotations to practice while Melanie counted out the beats. My first partner was Dustin. I held his hand and began my waltz with the embarrassing clutziness of someone who has no idea what she's doing.

The first stage of my uncomfortableness (is that a word?) was getting sweaty and still having to lift up my arms. The second was actually having to look at my partner. At first, I could stare at my feet, pretending to have trouble with the steps (who was pretending?).

Soon both Melanie and Davenport were correcting me, "Rachel, keep your head up! We want to see those eyes!"

I did everything in my power to keep my head up without actually looking at Dustin. One time I accidentally caught his eye, and it was the most awkward thing since coed wrestling.

The most entertaining part of the session was watching 6-foot-100, 30-year-old Margaret dance with 5-foot-9 teenage boys and try to appear interested.

Then it was freestyle or whatever. We sat down and the boys had to ask us to dance while Melanie played music. My first partner was Justin, who looked a little more human up close. I learned that he wanted to be in the Navy and didn't really like dancing. Next was Brandon who was going to Belmont University in Nashville and played the guitar. Then there was Thomas. He actually smelled good, and had an inviting smile. I made sure he knew I disapproved of his flirtatious manner and, being the skilled coquette that I am, brought every attempt at conversation to a screeching halt.

Thomas: *You're pretty good at this. You dance much?*
Me: *No.*
Thomas: *So you have an I.M.?*
Me: *Yeah.*
Thomas: *So can I, uh, I.M. you some time?*

Me: *Why?*

Then, I had another turn with Dustin, who I don't think liked me very much, because he only asked me to dance twice. I didn't really mind because he had sweaty hands.

I also learned that Zim was short for Zimran (it's supposedly from the Bible but sounds more like it came from "Star Trek"). I cannot remember talking about anything substantial with Zim, because it was sort of like trying to make conversation with a kindergartner.

Me: *So, do you go to Cotillion with the other boys here?*

Zim: *Yes, ma'am.*

Me: *And, um, are you still in high school?*

Zim: *Yes, ma'am, I am in 10th grade.*

Me: *You know, you really don't have to call me ma'am. I'm the same age as you.*

Zim: *No, ma'am, it's all right, I always do.*

Me: *No, please, you're making me feel old…*

And so it went for the duration of the dance. At some point we also did the cha-cha-slide (which was as appealing as it sounds) and the chicken dance, in which I am ashamed to admit I actually partook.

We then sat around and talked, and I found out that Dustin and Justin (rhyme!) were best friends and band members.

When we tried to show Brandon what kind of head shape he had, he jerked back and said quite seriously, "No, don't touch my hair." It was kind of funny and shamefully metro at the same time.

And then there was Katie, oh my! I happened to walk up to her during her conversation with Thomas and Justin.

Katie: *…yeah, you know what's a real turn-on? Kilts.*

Justin & Thomas: *Oh, yeah? Hoohoohoo, funny. And why do girls always like it when guys wear pink?*

Katie: *Ehmagawd, pink! I love it when guys wear pink! The best is pink kilts, it's like—Wooh! Clear the room!*

Justin (or **Thomas**, I forget)**:** *I hate it when they say that a real man wears pink.*

Thomas (or **Justin**)**:** *You know, a real man can wear pink and not say anything about it!*

Justin (or **Thomas**) **& Katie:** *Hoohoohoo, funny!*

Me: *You know, G.K. Chesterton once said, "Fallacies do not cease to be fallacies because they become fashions."*

You can imagine how that went over.

And then there was chatting with Dustin about how his sister used to be a Victoria's Secret model and he was looking into modeling, too. Again, funny and shamefully metro. I suggested he look into *Victor's Secret*. Quite clever, I thought, but he didn't laugh.

About three hours after we were supposed to be done, the boys had to leave, the girls had a fit, and I finally got to go to bed.

But not to sleep. Katie couldn't stop blabbering about how Justin said she had pretty eyes and Brandon said she danced like Gigi—who has *seen* that movie anyway?—and how cool it was that Justin and Dustin's names rhymed.

Anyway, I went to bed to the sound of Katie nattering, but not before I noticed I had gained some weight around the stomach area. I hoped the boys hadn't noticed.

Not that I cared if they did.

CHAPTER 13

SAY "CHEEES-Y"

When I woke up, Katie was still sound asleep. From experience, I knew she was a heavy sleeper and there was no need to be quiet, and so I stomped around the room getting dressed. When I stepped outside, it was just me and Asia. I suppose dancing was more exhausting than I thought.

Asia said to me, "Hey, I just heard that we can go eat breakfast early since today's the photo shoot and everyone's getting ready and stuff."

So *that's* what the others were doing.

I vaguely remembered Davenport saying something about a photo shoot, so we all could dress up and have individual pictures taken that we could hang above the mantle or something. I don't know, but it seemed like a good idea because the closest thing I have to a photo of me is half of my hair showing in the background of my sister's Facebook profile picture (sarcasm).

Asia and I had the dining room to ourselves, which made for a very peaceful morning. So we sat down and ate, and talked about the previous night, and how we both were surprised Davenport had enlisted boys to dance with us, and how we both sweat while dancing.

It turned out Asia was pretty cool to hang out with. I hadn't talked to her much because she had ended up being buddy-buddy with Evelyn. They referred to each other as "yin" and "yang" the whole time we were there.

When the conversation began to drag, I figured I'd try out some of the conversation tools I'd noticed Davenport using with some of the staff. I asked Asia if today was the last day of camp. I totally knew the answer (I'd been counting down the seconds), but I couldn't think of anything else to say. She replied that it was the last full day and that we would leave the next day.

"Do you wish it were longer, or are you looking forward to going home?" I asked.

"I could stay a few more days," she answered.

I tried not to fall out of my chair.

I figured out during my time with Asia that I never will be compatible with any carbon-based life form. What gave me that clue was when our conversation turned to the inordinate number of insects and worms at the camp.

Asia: *I hate worms. They make me crazy!*

Me: *Crazy? I was crazy once. They locked me in the dungeon and threw away the key. Then the worms came.*

I got that somewhere off the Internet, but apparently she'd never heard it, so you can imagine her reaction.

We got back to our rooms just as Katie and the other makeupified, big-haired girls were heading out to breakfast. I searched in my suitcase

71

for "The Sign of the Four" (Arthur Conan Doyle's second Sherlock Holmes novel, in case you're wondering) and read until Katie came and called me for class.

When we all gathered in the meeting room, Davenport gave me a look of elegantly restrained disapproval and said, "So, Rachel, were you not going to wear any makeup?"

Figures she would ask!

"Um…uh…well, actually, no…," I stumbled, "because…I didn't bring any, and I couldn't use Katie's 'cause it didn't match my skin tone."

Davenport smiled serenely, "That's not a problem. I have a whole case full of makeup and I'm sure some of it will work well with your skin."

Dang it! She had me cornered. "Umm, ohhh, uhhh, okay."

She pulled out a large leopard print briefcase from under her desk and flipped it open beside me. There were five different bottles of foundation, an assortment of mineral makeup, eye shadow, eyeliner, 17 different lipsticks, lip liner, brushes, and other stuff I couldn't identify. While the other girls headed outside to attend to their photos, Davenport put on her Chanel glasses and tried to find suitable makeup for my shiny, blemished face.

As she went to work, she couldn't resist saying in haughty teacher-mode, "Your face is so oily. You need to exfoliate."

My face, oily? How exactly was I supposed to respond to that? "Thanks, so is yours"?

I sat as close to perfectly still as I could while she keenly analyzed what she was up against, and then went to work with foundation, powder and rouge. Up close, I searched for deep lines, tiny wrinkles, blemishes or dark circles on her face. There were none. Her skin was as flawless as her demeanor.

Davenport's makeover of me seemed to take an eternity, but at least she didn't bring up the diamond shape thing again.

When she was finally done, Davenport gave me a long appraising look and said, "Oh, you look so pretty!"

I was excited to see what I looked like, so I ran to the bathroom to check myself out in the mirror. A 12-year-old girl who was trying to look like Marilyn Manson greeted me. I laughed quite rudely in her face until it registered that the girl I was looking at was, in fact, me. I kept on laughing nonetheless, because my reflection reminded me of Queen Elizabeth, who, when they found her dead, had six inches of makeup on her face.

It didn't look anything like me, and I started singing that reflection song from "Mulan." You know—

> *Whooooooo is that girl I see staring straight*
> *back at me?*
> *When will my reflection show who I am*
> *insiiiiIIIIIIIIIIIdde?* ♪

And after I was done with that, I made my way outside. Davenport marched—excuse me—*glided* behind me triumphantly, beaming at her creation.

Evelyn was posing for the photographer beside a live oak tree when Asia pointed to me, and all the other girls turned around to watch me come down the steps.

I heard, "Oh my gosh, your makeup looks so good!" and "Rachel— woo! Who did your makeup?"

I was dumbfounded, because I thought I looked terrible. Besides, I'm the sort of person who turns every compliment into an insult. In this case, when my campmates were telling me I looked so beautiful with the makeup on, I was tempted to say, "Ah, so you think I'm not beautiful *without* makeup?? You're saying that I am naturally ugly, is that it?!?" But I refrained.

The photographer's name was Ashley, and she seemed a little out of her element. She was probably used to working with an older audience in a less deserty setting. She sort of jumped around in a bubbly panic struggling to come up with an idea of what to do. First, she posed each of us by the oak tree, then in the fields with the big *plastic* flowers, and finally in the courtyard. She'd give us ridiculous instructions like, "Yes, good, keep doing that…bend over and pretend you're kissing the flower."

She even asked me to pucker my lips, and in those pictures I look like a bozo trying not to laugh.

Afterwards we went to our rooms to change and regroup. I was pleased when Katie acknowledged that the makeup Davenport put on me was too much, and she joined with me in making fun of Ashley and the photo shoot.

There was no lecture that afternoon, so we'd have extra time to get ready for the final dinner. I didn't have any makeup remover, but I managed to scrub all of it off with a washcloth, taking with it most of my epidermis in the process.

CHAPTER 12

ZIGZAG TOASTS

When I told my sister Sarah (the nail polish peeler) that I was writing a book, she kept badgering me to add her in as a pink-haired fairy princess of unicorns—exactly like the heroine of my story, she claimed, so I should have no trouble fitting her in. Right. I made no promises, and it felt good to have her asking me a favor for a change.

But back to my story.

Since I had absolutely nothing to do until dinner, I decided to get dressed early. I had 45 minutes until I actually had to be at the dining hall, so I tried to take my sweet time, just the way my mom always does when she has to get ready. I don't think I have to tell you that there was no way I was putting paint on my face again until I did an African rain dance (which didn't seem so absurd at the time since Texas was in the middle of another drought), so I was determined to look better than all the other girls WITHOUT any makeup (cue the smug, delusional grin). I did straighten my hair, moisturize my face, and repaint my nails. That took the better part of six minutes, so I spent the rest of the time wondering why I always did things three times as fast as everyone else.

It's sort of like when you finish your exam earlier than the rest of the class, and you look around at the other deathly-quiet students still brooding over answers, with their shoulder blades thrust out of their hunched backs, wondering if there was something you missed.

In this case, I knew what I had missed—makeup—so the analogy isn't watertight. I sighed and put on my black and pink beaded dress that was quite fashionable, if I do say so myself, along with my shoes (for visual poise) and a necklace.

Katie changed into a black dress with a blue sash that she had worn to a friend's graduation dance.

When we got to dinner, the others were decked out to the nines as well. Maggie had on some little strapless number that showed off her lifeguard tan lines. For some reason, I don't remember Erica's dress. Evelyn and Asia were color coordinated in black and white, but while Evelyn's was white with black polka dots, Asia's was a zebra print halter top with a V-neck deeper than the Grand Canyon. Everybody looked great that night.

The beginning was as frustratingly uneventful as the rest of our meals, with some very banal conversation and lame attempts at jokes. The only thing I remotely enjoyed was the filet mignon. (I was the only one who could pronounce it correctly. Smug grin again.) The pressure to maneuver the silverware properly, however, was even more intense than usual, as this was the final eating event of the week—the grand etiquette ball where I was probably going to lose both my glass slippers.

When the waitress served us some apple cider in a champagne glass, Davenport informed us that we had to make a toast to the person seated diagonally across from us. Then that person had to toast the next person, and so on, in a zigzag line down the table. Zigzag is a funny word. Zig. Zag. But I digress.

Davenport let her gaze trail across our group until it came to rest on me. "Why don't you go first, Rachel?" she warbled.

Of course. This was the final opportunity for her to put me on the spot.

Katie was sitting diagonally from me. I took a deep breath and began, "Katie..."

And my mind went blank.

I panicked for a moment, then managed, "...you're always so fun to be around, and very sweet and, um, kind."

More panic. I wondered if she could see the subtle fear in my eyes.

Somehow I plowed ahead, "You're so graceful and energetic, and, uh, everyone wants to be around you because you're so vivacious."

Relief! I raised my glass and everyone applauded and sipped their cider.

At the end of the zigzagging it was Erica's turn to toast me. It was surprisingly sweet. She basically said what everyone else had told me during the week—that I was intelligent, had a "good vocabulary," and "asked questions that everyone else was too lazy to ask." And then she added something about me being really polite and funny. Despite my better judgment, I actually liked the toast, because I could tell it was sincere.

Once we had gotten past the mandatory, sappy ones, we could make a toast to anyone else we wanted.

Most of the extra toasts went to Noelle, and to my great surprise, Noelle gave one to me.

"Rachel, it's been so fun getting to know you this past week…and you looked so beautiful at the photo shoot…"—I was actually feeling good for a second, but wait for it—"and the makeup looked so good on you. So I hope that you'll consider wearing makeup in the future because it enhances your natural features!"

She smiled and raised the glass, and everyone drank. I just smiled back blankly and mumbled thank you. I mean, what *could* I say? "No, Noelle, I most certainly will NOT consider wearing makeup in the future!!!!!"

Then it was time for dessert. We had Dutch chocolate cake and the conversation actually picked up a little after that. Evelyn took some pictures with her new camera, which are now on her Facebook page.

We had almost finished eating when Davenport rose and called us to attention. "Now then, ladies."

When we looked up, she was standing at the front of the table with a stack of papers in her hands. "This is the part when I hand the girls their graduating certificates, and they tell us what their favorite part of the week was."

I don't think I have to tell you that most of the girls' favorite part was the dancing because of—teehee—the boys. I said the photo shoot, but I was lying. I didn't have a favorite part. (I only had a *least* favorite part, and that was this game of having to pick a favorite part.)

Then it was Evelyn's turn. I get embarrassed again just thinking about it. She stood up and made a little speech, "I just want to thank Mrs. D for a great week here at camp, and I really enjoyed my experience here and, um, everything I've learned. And all of you guys have been so great and I liked that you"—here her eyes got red and watery—"wanted to make me better but didn't try to change *who* I am…sorry."

This is when she started crying, and everyone was shocked at first, and then responded. As for me, I was just shocked. Everyone ran up to give her a hug. I gave her one too, even though I didn't want to. Luckily, by the time I got up there, everyone else had a spot, so I just ended up hugging someone else who was hugging her.

After we all sat back down, a lot of the other girls were crying, too, and to my surprise, I saw Davenport wipe tears from her eyes.

When she said, "You know, at these final dinners we always get so emotional," we all laughed nervously.

Maggie was last, but after Evelyn's little speech, everything she came up with was pretty much irrelevant. No offense, Maggie.

Somehow the evening finally wrapped up. We all slowly got up and made our way out to the courtyard, where Evelyn and Katie took pictures of us in our dresses.

CHAPTER **15**

Sweet Freedom

Then we went to our rooms. Listening to Evelyn and Katie squawk on about how beautiful their pictures were was as intellectually stimulating as watching Dora the Explorer with my little brothers. (Seriously, does Dora really have to *yell* everything she says? "CAN YOU FIND THE *WAAAATERFAAAAALL*!!!????")

After 20 minutes of Katie exclaiming how she should be a model because she didn't realize how pretty she'd gotten, I was done. Then Asia came in and joined in the conversation, lauding Katie for her modeling skills (?!?!) and urging Noelle to participate. If I ever had any doubt of a Divine existence, it was banished when Noelle said no, and invited them to go swimming with her and the other girls. Which meant they would *leave the room!*

"Hey Rachel, we're going swimming, you wanna come?"

"Hmm? Oh, no thanks, I think I'm gonna watch my toenails grow instead."

At the slamming of the door I checked the clock on my phone. It was 10 p.m. Bedtime.

I went to sleep dreaming about slouching and passing dishes to the left, and about Katie being a road runner. The dream was pretty much like the cartoon—she ran around making the "meep meep" sound, and I unsuccessfully tried to catch her, ending up with a giant anvil falling on my head.

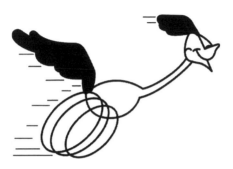

At some point I woke up to the sound of Katie returning to our room. She switched on the lights and I saw Asia standing in the doorway. I leaned over to look at the clock—10:54—and muttered, "You know, ya'll have to be back in, like, six minutes for curfew?"

Katie came out of the bathroom with the hair dryer and said, "Yeah, don't worry, go back to sleep."

They turned off the lights and left, and I fell asleep wondering what she needed the hair dryer for.

When I woke up again it was 5 a.m. I was cold, so I rolled over to get up and turn down the air conditioning. I expected to find Katie sleeping, but all I could see was her packed suitcase sitting on the edge of her bed. I jumped up and searched for her. She wasn't in the room. For some reason the first thing that occurred to me was that the guy from the "Texas Chainsaw Massacre" came to get her. I've never seen the movie and never will, but for some reason, that's what I imagined.

But then I thought, "Well that's just silly. If the dude came to get Katie, he would have probably taken me, too."

Then again, maybe my reputation had preceded me.

At first, it seemed like a miracle—she was gone!—but then I got angry because she had ignored curfew and I was going to have to look all around that desert for her. AND I knew if I didn't find her, this would somehow turn out to be *my fault*!

But then what occurred to me was, "Wait! Maybe she stayed in one of the other girls' rooms! That's probably it. But she should have at least left a note!!"

Still angry, I trudged over to her bed. Sure enough, hidden in the darkness lay a piece of paper: "Staying in Noelle's room. XOXO."

I was panting over it, still furious, but I don't remember why. Maybe it was because she wasn't actually gone, or maybe it was because she gave me such a fright. In any case, I went back to bed and fell asleep once more.

Two hours later I heard her stagger down the boardwalk, attempt to fiddle the key in the lock, and then moan, "Rachel?"

I flung open the door to find her slouched over, with bags under her eyes from exhaustion. I pointed an angry finger at her and exclaimed, "You scared the living DAYLIGHTS out of me!!!!"

She didn't know what I was talking about, so I explained the whole story (excluding the bit about it being a miracle that she was gone), and she thought it funny how I didn't find the note earlier. Then she collapsed onto her bed.

By then, I was no longer irritated. In fact, I was in the highest of spirits with the knowledge that today was the last day of my captivity. I almost skipped into the breakfast hall and loaded my plate with eggs and bacon. Only Davenport and Margaret were at the table, cordially chatting about boring, adult stuff.

Davenport turned to me. "Good morning, Rachel. It seems the other girls slept in this morning."

"Yes, I suppose they had a late night," I answered with smug superiority, loving the fact that I knew something she didn't.

"Well, it seems you're the most responsible one of the bunch."

I just about choked on my juice. Was that a compliment? Was she saying—miracle of miracles—something *good* about me?

I didn't know how to respond to this so I looked down embarrassed and stared at my lap until she began conversing with Margaret again.

Fortunately, Davenport soon excused herself, leaving Margaret and me to talk about my school curriculum and her major in philosophy. Margaret had a soft voice so I had to lean forward to hear her, but she was nice to talk to, even though I never did figure out why she had signed up for etiquette camp.

At some point, the other girls rushed in wearing their sweatpants and—God, pardon their sin!—no makeup. Looking a bit haggard with droopy eyes and tangled hair, they wolfed down their eggs, bacon and toast.

After breakfast we were instructed to finish packing and bring our suitcases to the classroom. That took another half hour.

When we finally all took our seats, Davenport stood in her usual spot at the front, scanned the room, peering into our souls, and intoned, "This has been a very special week for you girls."

I leaned back in my chair with a sigh because it was a sign that we would not be leaving anytime soon.

"I have seen a marked improvement in all of you."

Surely, I was excluded from that statement.

"Now, when you all leave today, you can go out into the world and be comfortable wherever you are."

She passed out a metal keychain to each of us, decorated with a compass and a slogan.

"The keychain says 'Lead by Example,'" she explained, "as you girls will do when you leave this camp, filled with such knowledge of places and settings."

Whatever that meant.

"People will look to you for example of what to do and how to act," she continued. "You will be leaders wherever you are."

I suppose this would be the part where soft, inspirational music begins to play and swell to a climactic finish as her final words, "You will be leaders…wherever you are…" reverberate through a wide-angle lens shot of all the girls leaving the room, marching out into the world to fulfill their destinies.

But that didn't happen.

Instead, Davenport suggested we exchange phone numbers and email addresses so we could "stay in touch" when we left. What everyone really did was add each other on Facebook so we could all get ahead at the "I have more friends on Facebook than you" competition.

It seemed like this was the time we were going to say our goodbyes, which I hate doing. And it's not for any cheesy "I hate change!" reasons. I don't like goodbyes because they make me feel uncomfortable, take too long, and there are so many routine platitudes you have to utter, things you *have* to say.

And, of course, there are all the awkward decisions: *Should I hug them or shake hands? But if I just shake hands, they will think I don't like them. Should I go for the hug first or wait for them to initiate it? What if I go to hug them and they go for the handshake instead?*

To resolve all that, I have initiated a policy to never touch anybody at all. And if anyone ventures to hug me, I'll start screaming and waving my arms frantically. It usually goes over really well.

But no one was really touchy-feely when we had to leave, and thankfully, everyone had exhausted their sappy, sentimental "boohoo-I'll miss you"-ness the night before, so I was able to digest my breakfast while we all waited for our parents to pick us up.

My mom drove up in her SUV pretty much on time, and at that moment she was the archangel Gabriel, halo and all.

I don't remember hugging anyone as I left; I was more like, "Nicemeetingyoumissyoubyeeeeeeeee" before I grabbed Katie's hand and dashed madly out of the building.

As our car pulled away, I began to shout, "FREEDOM! FREEDOM!"

My mom shushed me, "Rachel! They might hear you!"

But I didn't care. I was just ecstatic to be outta there.

EPILOGUE

I guess I could end on that note, but I'll follow us home and wait till later that night when Katie and I were jumping on the trampoline in my backyard. I found the trampoline particularly exhausting after my week-long eating fest, so I took short, low jumps to conceal how out of shape I was. We were jumping in circles, talking about camp, and suddenly it started to rain.

Katie: *Ha! This is so cool; is this actually rain?*

Me: *I don't know; it's a little more like a drizzle.*

The water had a cleansing effect; it seemed to wash away the stress and strain of the entire week.

Katie: *You know, Rachel, I'm glad I went to the camp with you.*

Me: *Why's that?*

Katie: *It was so much more fun with you. You make it easier for me to, like, make friends with people 'cause you smooth out the awkwardness and you're always so nice and funny.*

I looked around to see who she was talking to.

Katie: *Yeah, if I was there alone I'd probably not talk to anyone— or at least just be really shy.*

I looked around again.

We sat quietly next to each other for a few moments. Then, Katie turned to me.

Katie: *You know, Rachel, this stuff might actually be...like come in handy one of these days.*

Me (amused): *Oh yeah? How's that?*

Katie: *Like in college interviews and job interviews and...dressing appropriately and knowing when not to hug someone.*

Me: *Well...maybe.*

I hesitated to say she was right. But I was getting the feeling that she might be.

Katie: *And when you're meeting your boyfriend's parents, you'll know how to say hello and not look like a total loser in front of them.*

Well...

Katie: *And then there's that handshake block thing which might come in handy with the pervs at my school.*

We both laughed out loud. But she wasn't finished.

Katie: *You know, Rachel, you want to be a writer; you could write about this week or something!*

Me: *What, the week at camp?*

Katie: *Yeah, it could be like a story–slash–guide to etiquette.*

Me: *HA! Like* that's *ever going to happen!*

I sat there quietly and then it occurred to me: Katie had many wonderful qualities. She's kind and funny and always happy. She doesn't withhold a compliment and is always encouraging. She likes you and wants you to like her back.

And at that moment, I also realized that she probably wasn't the problem that whole week, neither was Davenport, nor was the camp itself; perhaps I was the problem.

I guess this is where I could get introspective and say that I saw people more clearly at that moment; that they weren't as annoying as

I make them out to be in my mind. I suppose I could say that even though we all are different, we all want the same things in life—acceptance, security, affirmation, attention—and we all go about trying to obtain them in our own, peculiar manner. And I guess I should say that was the moment I realized perhaps a change was called for.

Well, perhaps. But I'm not making any promises.

And as we lay there on the wet trampoline, chatting and laughing about our week, a pink-haired fairy princess (with peeled-off nail polish) flew by on her faithful, soft, gentle, white unicorn.

THE END

Acknowledgments

Thanks to Oleda Baker for her generous nature, encouragement, advice and guidance, which made this book possible. It would not have happened without her. Thanks also to Chris Angermann for taking a chance on publishing this book and for his extensive work during the editing process. I did not know editing could be so smooth and fun. I appreciate all his ideas and guidance.

A special thanks to my cousin Paul Feghali, who contributed the Furby and diamond head illustrations.

Final Touch Finishing School is located in Texas. All etiquette tips listed in this book were obtained directly from its summer camp program or from "The Etiquette Handbook Guide," developed by the school's founder and director, Deborah King. You may find more information about the camp, as well as other etiquette programs the school offers, at www.finaltouchschool.com.

Reflection
from Walt Disney Pictures' MULAN
Music by Matthew Wilder
Lyrics by David Zippel
Walt Disney Music Company
All rights reserved, used by permission
Reprinted by permission of Hal Leonard Corporation

About the Author

Rachel Aboukhair lives in Burleson, Texas with her parents, older sister and two younger brothers. When she's not being grumpy she enjoys reading, hiding from people she doesn't like, playing Scrabble, and avoiding talking about where she's going to college. She plays the f lute and piano, but only because her mom makes her. She also likes traveling to other countries and reading books nobody else likes, and is currently working on the next "Grumpy Girl" adventure guide.